# How to Cope with Social Anxiety:

## Overcoming the Challenges of Social Phobia

By Diane Carla

## Table of Contents

Chapter 1: The Truth about Anxiety

Chapter 2: What are Phobias?

Chapter 3: Anxiety Disorders

Chapter 4: What is Social Anxiety Disorder?

Chapter 5: Tips and Strategies for Living with Social Phobia

Chapter 6: Developing Communication Skills for Real life Situations

Chapter 7: Treatment and Therapy for Social Anxiety Disorder

# Chapter 1: The Truth about Anxiety

Why do so many people these days appear so stressed and anxious? It's a familiar question, among mental health specialists and laypeople alike, but there's a case to be made that it's precisely upside down. How come there's anybody who isn't crippled by anxiety, every hour of every day? After all, anxiety flourishes in settings of uncertainty – and presently the world is filled with possible risks we don't completely comprehend and can't manage.

Most of us simply have to take it on faith that aircraft won't fall out of the sky, or that the milk in our fridge won't give us listeria. Sudden, unexpected moves in the global financial system threaten to wreck anyone's livelihood at any time.

Some definitions may assist here. "Stress", as psychologists prefer to phrase it, denotes a rapid reaction to an external demand, and a reasonable amount may be a desirable thing: unstressed individuals never study for examinations, or fulfill job deadlines. In most ordinary circumstances, as the external pressure quits, so does the stress. This implies that by far the easiest approach to cope with stress, wherever feasible, is to deal with whatever's upsetting you full on – to face the tough piece of work, to speak to the person you've fallen out with – or, failing that, to separate or divert yourself from its cause. (Persistent and chronic stress demands a different technique.)

But anxiety is a unique type of psychological reaction to stress, and it's typically considerably more complicated. As the Australian novelist Sarah Wilson points out in her combination memoir and anxiety self-help handbook, First, We Make the Beast Beautiful, the issue isn't just that there are a lot of reasons to feel nervous. It's also because, perversely, society encourages some anxious habits, such as being frantically busy and driven – whereas the "reward" for managing to free oneself from worry can be a reputation for sloth, complacency, or exhibiting inadequate care about the status of the world. Then there's the fact that anxiety is self-reinforcing: once you're feeling worried, you're prepared to seek other things to be concerned about – even, as if that vicious loop weren't terrible enough, your worry itself.

Anxiety, at its core, isn't an odd psychiatric abnormality, but a basic element of human functioning. "Anxiety", of course, is also the term for a family of formal psychiatric diseases. But it's a disease that makes it exceptionally evident that the border between "mental illness" and "ordinary human distress" is a subjective one, relying as much on cultural standards as on science. The major reason "generalized anxiety disorder" is so much more widespread today is because it was only classified as a condition in psychiatry's bible, the Diagnostic and Statistical Manual of Mental Disorders, in 1980. (If you feel "keyed up or on edge", or have "difficulty concentrating", it's conceivable you qualify.)

And one key reason it grew from 2001 onwards was a deliberate media effort by GlaxoSmithKline when it got US authorization to sell its antidepressant Paxil (Seroxat in the UK) in the treatment of anxiety. “Local newscasts throughout [the United States] stated that as many as 10 million Americans suffered from an unrecognized disease,” journalist Brendan Koerner has written. “Viewers were encouraged to look for the symptoms: restlessness, weariness, irritation, muscular tension, nausea, diarrhea, and sweating …”

To be clear, none of this is to indicate that persons with a documented anxiety condition don’t have a legitimate disease, or that medicine isn’t frequently part of the solution: “The essential foundation for an anxiety disorder, or when anxiety becomes a clinical condition, is when anxiety rules our lives, rather than us being able to regulate our worry,” cxplains Robert Edelmann, emeritus professor of forensic and clinical psychology at the University of Roehampton. But it’s also a reminder that worry, at its core, isn't an odd psychiatric abnormality, but a basic element of human functioning. The difficulty, adds the psychology writer James Clear, author of Atomic Habits, is that it's a reaction nature gave us for a setting dramatically different from today.

All worry includes a kernel of good news: you wouldn't feel concerned if there weren't the prospect of things going well

Prehistoric humans lived in an "instant-return environment", as other animals currently do: their moment-to-moment decisions mattered because of the immediate impact they made. You saw a predator and felt a surge of anxiety, which motivated you to evade it. Or you were dangerously hungry, and fear focused your attention on swiftly getting food. Once the danger was handled, the worry would dissipate. But contemporary people live in a "delayed-return environment". We are paid for our labor at the end of the week or month; we study for educational degrees that take years. When we save money – or don't – the ramifications could not be realized for decades. And so the anxiousness has nowhere to go. Instead, it collects and curdles.

This helps explain why national and international news events are typically such broad causes of personal worry, especially of the clinical variety. Some individuals are influenced in immediate, unmistakable ways. But even if you eventually won't be, you'll have no way of knowing that for some time. Moreover, it frequently seems like there's nothing you can do in reaction — no comparison to the ancient hunter-gatherer option to start running away or begin hunting for food. When no creative activity appears conceivable, we turn to anxiety and rumination, which seem somehow useful, even when they aren't. One reaction to the anxiety of being immersed in a 24-hour news cycle "is that people try to find out more information because anxiety is about a lack of control and they believe that having more information will make them feel more in control", says the American therapist Lori

Gottlieb, author of the forthcoming book Maybe You Should Talk to Someone. "But it doesn't - it only makes them feel more anxious."

This is why most non-pharmaceutical solutions to anxiety, whatever its cause, involve the limited and realistic exertion of control: figuring out what constructive actions you can take, and taking them while refraining from struggling to control things you can't, which is a recipe for additional anxiety. (This is the "dichotomy of control", a distinction dating to the Stoics of ancient Greece and Rome.) You can't personally guarantee a comfortable retirement, or long-term physical health, let alone the optimal relationship between Britain and the rest of Europe. But you can determine what you can afford to save, and monitor your saving. You can exercise a few times a week, and eat more leafy greens. You can take local, tangible political action. Whether or whether you end up attaining your intended objective, your anxiety levels will almost surely diminish.

Finally, it's worth recognizing – as the Danish philosopher Søren Kierkegaard observed in The Concept of Anxiety back in 1844 – that all anxiety contains a kernel of good news: you wouldn't feel anxious in the first place if you had no freedom, and if there weren't at least the possibility of things turning out well. "One would not worry if there were no possibility whatsoever," remarked the psychologist Rollo May, citing Kierkegaard. If you knew with full confidence that life from now on would bring only failure and defeat, you may easily be miserable, but you wouldn't be on edge. Anxiety is the sense of knowing that life may provide achievement, happiness, and pleasure, but with the anxiety that you don't know how to assure that's what will happen. And although acute anxiety may be a terrible disease, necessitating treatment, some feeling of uncertainty about the future is surely part of what makes life worth living. If you ever genuinely managed to rule out the chance for any terrible shocks, you'd discover that you'd ruled out the possibility of any nice ones, too.

.

Anxiety is not the same as fear, yet they are frequently used interchangeably. Anxiety is regarded as a future-oriented, long-acting reaction largely focused on a dispersed danger, while terror is an acceptable, present-oriented, and short-lived response to a clearly recognized and precise threat.

# Chapter 2: What are Phobias?

A phobia is an uncontrolled, unreasonable, and permanent dread of a given thing, circumstance, or activity. This dread may be so intense that a person may go to considerable efforts to escape the cause of this anxiety. One reaction might be a panic attack. This is a sudden, acute dread that lasts for many minutes. It occurs when there is no genuine threat.

If a phobia gets particularly severe, a person may structure their life around avoiding the item that's giving them distress. As well as constraining their day-to-day existence, it may also cause a lot of anguish.

Who is impacted by phobias?

About 19 million Americans have one or more phobias that vary from minor to severe. Phobias may arise in early infancy. But they are generally first spotted between ages 15 and 20. They impact both men and women equally. But males are more likely to seek therapy for phobias.

What creates phobias?

Research reveals that both hereditary and environmental factors contribute to the genesis of phobias. Certain phobias have been connected to an extremely poor first experience with the dreaded thing or scenario. Mental health professionals don't sure whether this initial interaction is required or if phobias might just emerge in those who are inclined to have them.

What are the primary forms of phobias?

Specific phobia

What is a Specific phobia?
Specific phobia is an excessive dread of an item or scenario that normally isn't harmful.

Examples may include a dread of:

- Flying (believing the aircraft may crash)
- Dogs (fearing the dog may bite or attack)
- Closed-in areas (fear of being imprisoned) (fear of being trapped)
- Tunnels (fearing a collapse)
- Heights (fear of falling)

What are the features of a specific phobia?

People with particular phobias recognize that their dread is intense. But they can't conquer it. The issue is recognized only when the particular fear interferes with regular activities of the school, job, or family life.

There is no known cause, however, they appear to run in families. They are also seen significantly more commonly in women. If the object of the fear is simply to avoid, persons with phobias may not seek therapy. Sometimes, though, people may make significant professional or personal choices to avoid a circumstance that involves the cause of the phobia.

Treatment for Specific phobia

When phobias interfere with a person's life, therapy may assist. For certain phobias, cognitive-behavioral therapy (CBT) plus exposure treatment is indicated. In exposure therapy, individuals are progressively exposed to what frightens them until the fear begins to disappear. Relaxation and breathing techniques can assist to relieve discomfort.

Social phobia

What is social phobia?

Social phobia is an anxiety condition in which a person has substantial anxiety and discomfort connected to a fear of being embarrassed, humiliated, or despised by others in social or performance circumstances. Even when they manage to tackle this anxiety, persons with social phobia usually:

- Feel highly worried before the event or excursion

- Feel severely uncomfortable during the event or excursion
- Have lasting bad sentiments after the event or excursion

Social phobia typically arises with the following:

- Public speaking
- Meeting folks
- Dealing with authoritative figures
- Eating in public
- Using public bathrooms

What are the features of social phobia?

Although this illness is commonly thought of as shyness, they are not the same. Shy individuals might be highly nervous among others, but they don't have acute anxiety in anticipating a social setting. Also, they don't always avoid settings that make them feel self-conscious. In contrast, people with social phobia are not necessarily shy at all but can be completely at ease with some people most of the time.

Most people with social phobia will try to avoid situations that cause distress.

## Diagnosing social phobia

Social phobia is identified when the fear or avoidance substantially interferes with normal routines, or is highly disturbing.

Social phobia affects regular living, interfering with employment or social interactions. It commonly runs in families and may occur together with sadness or drinking. Social phobia generally originates in the early teens or even earlier.

## Treatment for social phobia

People with social phobia generally find relief when treated with cognitive-behavioral therapy, pharmaceuticals, or a combination of both.

## Agoraphobia

What is agoraphobia?

Agoraphobia is the dread of having a panic attack at a place or scenario from which escape may be hard or embarrassing.

The anxiety of agoraphobia is so acute that panic episodes are not rare. People with agoraphobia generally strive to avoid the area or source of their dread. Agoraphobia entails anxiety about circumstances like the following:

- Being alone outside his or her house
- Being at home alone
- Being in a throng
- Traveling in a vehicle
- Being in an elevator or on a bridge

People with agoraphobia often avoid crowded locations including streets, crowded shops, churches, and theaters.

What are the features of agoraphobia?

Most persons with agoraphobia obtain it after initially having a series of panic episodes. The assaults happen randomly and without notice, and make it hard for a person to foresee what may provoke the response. This unpredictability of the panic drives the sufferer to anticipate future panic attacks and, ultimately, dread any scenario in which an attack may happen. As a consequence, they avoid entering into any area or circumstance where past panic attacks have transpired.

People with the condition can become so incapacitated that they physically feel they cannot leave their houses. Others who have agoraphobia, do venture into potentially "phobic" circumstances, but only with significant discomfort, or when accompanied by a close friend or family member.

People with agoraphobia may also have melancholy, weariness, stress, alcohol or drug misuse issues, and compulsive disorders, making therapy vital.

## Chapter 3: Anxiety Disorders

An anxiety disorder is a sort of mental health issue. If you have an anxiety condition, you may react to particular objects and circumstances with fear and dread. You may also have physical indicators of anxiety, such as a racing pulse and sweating.

It's natural to experience some anxiousness. You may feel anxious or worried if you have to face an issue at work, go to an interview, take a test or make an important choice. And worry may even be useful. For example, anxiety helps us identify risky circumstances and concentrates our attention, so we remain safe.

But an anxiety disorder goes beyond the ordinary anxiousness and minor worry you may experience from time to time. An anxiety disorder arises when:

Anxiety interferes with your capacity to operate.

You typically overreact when anything provokes your emotions.
You can't control your reactions to events.
Anxiety problems may make it difficult to get through the day. Fortunately, there are various effective therapies for anxiety disorders.

Who is at risk for anxiety disorders?

A combination of genetic and environmental variables may boost a person's risk for developing anxiety disorders. You may be at increased risk if you have or had:

- Certain personality qualities, such as shyness or behavioral inhibition – feeling uncomfortable with, and avoiding, unknown individuals, circumstances, or places.
- Stressful or painful occurrences in early infancy or maturity.
- Family history of anxiety or other mental health issues.

- Certain health disorders include thyroid difficulties and cardiac arrhythmias (unusual heartbeats) (unusual heart rhythms).

Anxiety problems occur more commonly in women. Researchers are still exploring why that occurs. It may arise from women's hormones, particularly those that change during the month. The hormone testosterone may have a role, too – males have more, and it may relieve anxiety. It's also plausible that women are less inclined to seek therapy, thus the anxiety escalates.

What are the forms of anxiety disorders?
There are various forms of anxiety disorders, including:

Generalized anxiety disorder (GAD) (GAD).
Panic disorder.
Phobias.
Separation anxiety.
Other mental health diseases share similarities with anxiety disorders. These include

post-traumatic stress disorder and obsessive-compulsive disorder.

What is generalized anxiety disorder (GAD)?
With GAD, you may experience intense and unreasonable anxiety and tension – even if there's nothing to induce these sensations. Most days, you may worry a lot about many subjects, including health, job, education, and relationships. You may feel that the concern extends from one issue to the next.

Physical symptoms of GAD might include restlessness, difficulties focusing, and sleeping issues.

What is a panic disorder?

If you have a panic disorder, you have acute, abrupt panic episodes. These episodes frequently involve greater, more powerful sensations than other forms of anxiety disorders.

The sensations of panic may start quickly and unexpectedly or they may come from a trigger, such as approaching a scenario you dread. Panic attacks may mimic heart attacks. If there's any likelihood you're having a heart attack, go to the emergency department. It's preferable to err on the side of caution and have a healthcare expert check you.

During a panic attack, you may experience:

- Sweating.
- Heart palpitations (feeling like your heart is thumping) (feeling like your heart is pounding).
- Chest discomfort.
- Feeling of choking, which might make you fear you're having a heart attack or "going crazy."

Panic attacks are quite unpleasant. People with panic disorder typically spend a lot of time worrying about the next panic episode. They also strive to avoid circumstances that can provoke an assault.

What is separation anxiety disorder?

This illness mainly occurs in youngsters or teenagers, who may worry about being away from their parents. Children with separation anxiety disorder may worry that their parents may be injured in some manner or not return as promised. It occurs a lot in preschoolers. But older children and adults who undergo a distressing incident may develop a separation anxiety disorder as well.

How frequent are anxiety disorders?

Anxiety disorders are the most frequent mental health issues in the U.S. They impact around 40 million Americans. They happen to almost 30% of people at some time. Anxiety disorders most typically develop in infancy, adolescence, or early adulthood.

How do anxiety issues influence children?

It's common for youngsters to experience some level of anxiety, concern, or dread at particular stages. For example, a youngster may feel terrified by a thunderstorm or barking dog. A teenager can become nervous about an approaching exam or school dance.

But occasionally, youngsters approach these moments with tremendous dread or they can't stop thinking about all the concerns related to one of these occurrences. None of your comforts may assist. These youngsters typically become "stuck" on their problems. They have a hard time conducting their normal tasks, such as going to school, playing, and falling asleep. They're hesitant to attempt anything new.

When thinking about your child's anxiety levels, "getting stuck" is crucial. It distinguishes the typical anxieties of children from an anxiety illness that requires expert assistance. If the fear or stress interferes with your child's ability to function, it may be time to seek assistance

## SYMPTOMS AND CAUSES

What causes anxiety disorders?

Anxiety disorders are like other kinds of mental diseases. They don't arise from human weakness, character defects, or difficulties with upbringing. But experts don't know precisely what causes anxiety problems. They think a combination of variables has a role:

Chemical imbalance: Severe or long-lasting stress may affect the chemical balance that determines your mood. Experiencing a lot of stress over a long time might develop into an anxiety condition.

Environmental factors: Experiencing a trauma could induce an anxiety disorder, particularly in someone who has inherited a greater risk to start.

Heredity: Anxiety problems tend to run in families. You may inherit them from one or both parents, like eye color.

What are the signs of an anxiety disorder?

Symptoms vary based on the sort of anxiety problem you have. General signs of an anxiety condition include:

Physical symptoms:

Cold or sweaty hands.
Dry mouth.
Heart palpitations.
Nausea.
Numbness or tingling in hands or feet.
Muscle stress.
Shortness of breath.

Mental symptoms:

Feeling panic, anxiety, and discomfort.
Nightmares.
Repeated thoughts or flashbacks of unpleasant occurrences.
Uncontrollable, compulsive thoughts.

Behavioral symptoms:

Inability to remain motionless and peaceful.

Ritualistic actions, such as washing hands frequently.

Trouble sleeping.

How can I tell if my kid has an anxiety disorder?

Anxiety-related issues in children have four basic aspects. The anxiety:

- Is often a fear or preoccupation that interferes with the capacity to enjoy life, get through the day, or finish duties.
- Is perplexing to both the youngster and parents.
- Does not improve following rational answers to address the fears.
- Is curable.

# Chapter 4: What is Social Anxiety Disorder?

We all know the sensation of being scared or uncomfortable in a social environment. Maybe you've clammed up while meeting someone new or had sweaty hands before delivering a large presentation. Public speaking or stepping into a roomful of strangers isn't exactly exhilarating for anyone, but most individuals can get through it.

If you have a social anxiety disorder, which is also known as social phobia, the stress of these circumstances is too much to take. You could, for example, shun any social interaction because things that most people consider "normal" — like making small chats and eye contact — make you so uncomfortable. All elements of your life, not just the social ones, might start to come apart.

Social anxiety disorder affects roughly 5.3 million individuals in the United States. The typical age it starts is between age 11 and 19 — the teenage years. It's one of the most prevalent mental conditions, so if you have it, there's hope. The challenging part is being able to ask for assistance. Here's how to recognize whether your social quiet has gone beyond shyness to a point where you need to consult a doctor.

When Does It Happen?

In some persons with social anxiety disorder, the dread is restricted to one or two specific circumstances, such as speaking in public or beginning a conversation. Others are exceedingly apprehensive and terrified of any social circumstance.

Anyone with a social anxiety disorder might experience it in various ways. But here are some frequent circumstances that individuals seem to have difficulties with:

- Talking to strangers
- Speaking in public\sDating
- Making eye contact
- Entering rooms
- Using public bathrooms
- Going to parties
- Eating in front of other people
- Going to school or work
- Starting discussions

Some of these circumstances may not present an issue for you. For example, making a speech may be simple, but going to a party can be a nightmare. Or you might be fantastic at one-on-one interactions but lousy at going into a packed classroom.

All socially anxious persons have distinct reasons for fearing specific situations. But in general, it's an overpowering dread of:

- Being scrutinized or monitored by others in social circumstances
- Being ashamed or humiliated — and displaying it by flushing, sweating, or shaking
- Accidentally insulting someone
- Being the focus of attention

What Does It Feel Like?

Again, the experience may be different for everyone, but if you have social anxiety and you're in a difficult scenario, you may feel:

- Very self-conscious in social circumstances

- A persistent, strong, and chronic anxiety about being evaluated by others
- Shy and uncomfortable while being observed (making a presentation, chatting in a group) (giving a presentation, talking in a group)
- Hesitant to speak to people
- The urge to avoid eye contact

You also could have bodily symptoms such as:

- Rapid heartbeat
- Muscle tension
- Dizziness and lightheadedness
- Blushing
- Crying\sSweating
- Stomach problems and diarrhea
- Inability to catch a breath
- An "out-of-body" feeling

You may start feeling symptoms and become apprehensive just before an event, or you can spend weeks thinking about it. Afterward, you might spend a lot of time and mental energy thinking about how you behaved.

## What Causes It?

No one item causes social anxiety disorder. Genetics likely has something to do with it: If you have a family member with social phobia, you're more at risk of getting it, too. It might also be connected to having an overactive amygdala — the portion of the brain that governs your fear response.

Social anxiety disorder normally comes at about 13 years of age. It may be connected to a history of abuse, bullying, or taunting. Shy kids are also more prone to become socially anxious adults, as are children with domineering or controlling parents. If you have a physical problem that attracts attention to your look or voice, it might induce social anxiety, too.

## How Can It Affect Your Life?

Social anxiety conditions inhibit you from enjoying your life. You'll avoid circumstances that most people consider "normal." You could even have a hard time comprehending how others can manage them so simply.

When you avoid all or most social interactions, it damages your connections. It may also lead to:

- Low self-esteem
- Negative thoughts
- Depression
- Sensitivity to criticism
- Poor social skills that don't develop

## What Can I Do About Social Anxiety Disorder?

If your social anxiety hinders you from doing activities you want or need to do, or from establishing or retaining friends, you may require therapy.

Talk about your thoughts and worries with a doctor or therapist who has expertise with social anxiety disorder. They will be able to assess whether you have typical social anxiety or if you require therapy.

## How Is Social Anxiety Disorder Treated?

Prescription medicine and behavioral therapy are the two effective therapies for social anxiety disorder. You may get both at the same time. Here is some information about each:

Medications: For some, taking a prescription drug may be a simple and successful therapy for social anxiety disorder. The medications operate by minimizing the painful and frequently humiliating symptoms. Sometimes medicine may substantially lower your symptoms or perhaps remove them. Others individuals may not respond to a specific drug, and some aren't benefited at all. There is no way to forecast whether a drug would benefit you or not.

Sometimes, you must test numerous before finding one that works.

The Food and Drug Administration (FDA) has authorized four drugs for a social anxiety disorder: Paxil, Zoloft, Luvox, and Effexor. Although these are the only drugs licensed expressly for the illness, other medications may be used effectively, too.

The benefit of drugs is that they may be highly effective, and are given only once a day. But there are some drawbacks.

First, medicine simply cures symptoms. If you stop taking medication, your symptoms might reappear. Second, some people get adverse effects from anxiety drugs. They may include headaches, stomachaches, nausea, and sleep problems.

Also, the FDA-approved drugs for social anxiety disorder, like any pharmaceuticals that are also used to treat depression, have a warning from the FDA. The FDA says the drugs may induce or exacerbate suicidal thoughts or actions in young individuals under age 24. Therefore, youths who take these drugs should be examined attentively for changes in thoughts about suicide.

For many individuals, the benefits of drugs exceed the dangers. You and your doctor must consider the option.

If you take medication for social anxiety disorder, contact your doctor immediately if you experience any adverse effects, including feeling sad and depressed. And never stop taking any anxiety medication without talking to your doctor first. Suddenly quitting an anxiety medication may create major negative effects.

Behavioral treatment: Behavioral therapy with a skilled therapist may help you discover and modify the thinking that makes you uncomfortable in social settings.

A kind of behavioral treatment called exposure therapy is widely used for social anxiety disorder. Exposure therapy works by progressively exposing you to social circumstances that are unpleasant and waiting until you feel comfortable. During this process, your brain is learning that a social scenario you were terrified of is not that horrible.

Most therapists who perform exposure therapy begin with minor exposures to unpleasant circumstances, then go on to more challenging exposures until you feel comfortable. The benefit of this treatment is that you are addressing the actual issue, not simply the symptoms of social anxiety disorder. So if you discontinue behavioral treatment, the risk of your symptoms returning is less probable.

## Other treatments

Other methods have also been tested for treating social anxiety disorder. They include:

Relaxation therapy: With this therapeutic method, you learn skills for relaxing such as breathing exercises and meditation. Although relaxation therapy may assist with certain particular social phobias, it is not considered an effective treatment for generalized anxiety disorder.

Beta-blockers: These drugs were initially used to treat high blood pressure or other cardiac conditions. Yet beta-blockers are also beneficial for treating certain persons with a particular sort of social phobia termed "performance social anxiety." This is when you are terrified of performing, like delivering a public speech. Beta-blockers are not useful for treating general social anxiety disorder. But they may help if fear of a specific circumstance, occurring at a specific, predictable time — like giving a speech to a class — is your problem.

## When Should I Talk to My Doctor About Social Anxiety?

First, it's important to know that you are not abnormal if you have social anxiety. Many individuals have it. If you experience abnormally high anxiety and concern about social settings, discuss it freely with your doctor about treatment. If left untreated, social anxiety disorder may lead to depression, drug or alcohol issues, school or job troubles, and a poor quality of life.

# Chapter 5: Tips and Strategies for Living with Social Phobia

Social anxiety disorder (SAD) assistance may come in various ways. Although medication is accessible and effective for SAD, it is estimated that only 35 percent of patients with the illness ever undergo treatment.

While not a replacement for professional therapy, for people who may otherwise get no care, self-help is an excellent beginning point.

The self-help solutions for social anxiety disorder listed here may be employed at home to conquer your symptoms.

Social Coping

A smart first step to managing social anxiety disorder is to identify the social skills that might need a little more practice. If you work on improving them, it may help you manage the thoughts and feelings that occur with social anxiety disorder.

## Assertiveness

Many persons with social anxiety disorder lack assertiveness and might benefit from learning to become more forceful via self-help tactics.

Practice being more assertive by conveying your requirements in a calm and relaxed manner that respects the needs of others. Usually, this takes the form of "I" statements such as "I feel wounded when you don't answer my phone calls." Learning to say no is also a crucial element of being assertive and a skill that most individuals with social anxiety struggle with.

## How to Be More Assertive When You Have SAD

### Nonverbal Communication

Improving your nonverbal communication abilities is another area in which you may utilize self-help tactics if you suffer from social anxiety.

Most persons with social anxiety tend to assume a "closed-off" position; you may do this without even recognizing it. Learning how to have a comfortable posture (e.g. hands at your sides, excellent eye contact) encourages people to react favorably to you and helps you look more accessible. 5

Developing body confidence in this manner can assist you to become more confident in social situations.

Verbal Communication

In addition to having a calm body posture, learning how to initiate conversations, keep them going, and listen carefully are abilities that you may improve via self-help tactics.

As an example, one simple strategy for engaging a group of people in discussion is to listen first and then offer a remark about what they are currently talking about. For example, "Are you talking about the election results? I couldn't believe them either."

Expose yourself to as many chances as possible to strengthen your verbal communication talents. Practice being a good listener, asking open-ended questions, and sharing experiences about yourself so that people may come to know you better.

## How to Socialize When You Have Social Anxiety Disorder

### Telling Others About Your Social Anxiety

It's probable your closest relatives and friends already have an understanding of your social anxiety. If you want to tell someone, in particular, send a message indicating there is something you'd want to discuss and organize a time at a peaceful spot to chat.

If you are too frightened to describe your predicament, jot down a summary of what you've been experiencing. It's essential to disclose your symptoms so that the other person may develop an understanding of what you are going through.

Remember that not everyone will know the ins and outs of social anxiety disorder; some individuals may need some aid to grasp what they're going through.

## Emotional Coping

Fear and negative thoughts are two of the most typical feelings when you experience social anxiety. A few easy tactics might help you overcome them.

## Deep Breathing

Having social anxiety indicates that you probably have significant emotional responses in social settings. One strategy to lessen these worried emotions is for your body to be in a calm condition. When your body is relaxed, your breathing is calm and natural, and your mind is free of negative ideas, making it is simpler to appreciate being with people.

You probably breathe too fast in anxiety-provoking circumstances, which in turn makes your other anxiety symptoms worse.

Below are some methods to control your nervous and shallow breathing.

## How to Practice Deep Breathing

Count the number of breaths that you take in one minute (count an inhalation and exhale as one) (count an inhale and exhale as one). Make a note of this number. The typical individual will take 10 to 12 breaths each minute.

Focus on your breathing. Inhale via your nose and exhale through your mouth. Take deep breaths from your diaphragm instead of short breaths from your chest. Inhale for 3 seconds and exhale for 3 seconds (use a watch or clock with a second hand) (use a watch or clock with a second hand). As you exhale, think "relax" and release tension in your muscles. Continue breathing in this manner for 5 minutes.

Count your breaths per minute again and check whether the number has gone down.

Practice this breathing method a few times each day while you are already calm. It may assist to

start practicing when you first wake up and before you go to sleep.
When in social settings, be sure that you are breathing in the manner that you rehearsed. In time, this technique of breathing may become more automatic.

## Reducing Negative Thinking

If you live with social anxiety, you probably misunderstand words or facial expressions produced by other people, which adds to your emotional responses. For instance, there are two frequent thinking patterns that might add to your worry.

Mind Reading: You assume that you know what other people are thinking about you (e.g. "Everyone can see how worried I am"). (e.g. "Everyone can see how anxious I am.").

Personalizing: You think that the behavior of others is connected to you (e.g. "He seems bored, I shouldn't have asked him to this movie.").

The ideas that you have are so habitual that you probably aren't even aware you are having them. Below are some strategies to better manage your negative thoughts.

## How to Reduce Negative Thoughts

Think back to a recent social scenario in which you felt apprehensive. Write down what your negative thoughts were before, during, and after the occurrence.

Ask yourself questions to confront your negative thinking. For example, if your negative automatic thinking was "People are yawning, they must think that I am boring," ask yourself "Could there be another explanation?" In this scenario, your alternate perspective may be "It probably had nothing to do with me, they were simply weary."

Try to recognize the habitual negative ideas that you have before, during, and after dreaded social encounters, and fight them with alternatives.

Overcome Negative Thinking When You Have SAD

Facing Your Fears

Avoiding fearful circumstances may minimize your emotional responses in the short term, but in the long run, it significantly restricts your life. In addition, the number of scenarios that you dread expands as your fear gets more comprehensive. On the other hand, gradual exposure to social events paired with relaxation methods can assist to minimize the anxiety and emotional responses that you connect with such circumstances.

There are techniques to overcome avoidance. To start, pick the top 10 scenarios that you avoid. For each circumstance on the list, break it down into a sequence of stages, increasing in severity.

For example, if you are frightened of being the focus of attention, your steps may look like this:

- Tell an amusing tale about yourself to a group of individuals who you know well.
- Tell an amusing tale about yourself to a group of individuals who you don’t know well.
- Voice your true opinion to a group of friends.
- Voice your true opinion to a group of strangers.
- Make a toast at dinner with people whom you know well.
- Make a toast at dinner with people whom you don't know well.
- Practice each step as much as you need to before going on to the next. If you sense anxiousness, question your negative thoughts and utilize the slow breathing method to calm down.

Note that the particular list you produce will depend on your worries. For example, you could feel more terrified about speaking in front of individuals you know well vs a throng of strangers. In this scenario, you would invert things on the list.

## Day-to-Day Strategies

Below are some tips to help you cope with social anxiety on a day-to-day basis, such as while at work or attending school.

Tell your employer so that you can receive accommodations or supports in the workplace.

Arrive to meetings early so you can meet people one by one as they arrive.

Make a list of questions to ask your teacher or supervisor and start with the least anxiety-provoking ones.

Keep informed on current events so that you will be able to join in a small chat.

Avoid using alcohol to overcome inhibitions.

Choose a career that you love so that even the toughest portions of work in terms of your social anxiety will seem worth it.

Make new friends by meeting people, expressing compliments, and beginning short chats.

Get frequent exercise, consume nutritious food, and avoid coffee and sweets to lessen your anxiety.

## Mistakes to Avoid

There are a lot of frequent blunders that individuals make while attempting to overcome social anxiety using self-help tactics. Avoiding these blunders will guarantee that you aren't making matters worse.

Never attempt to manage your anxiousness. The more you regard it as something horrible that has to be eradicated, the more concentrated you will be on it and the harder it will be to lessen.

Don't concentrate on being flawless. Instead, concentrate on accepting worst-case possibilities and then move backward from there.

Never embrace social anxiety as a personality feature. While you could be an introvert or have a propensity to be shy, social anxiety disorder is a mental health condition that does not define who you are. It is possible to conquer your anxiety and live a fulfilled life.

While there is some evidence that cannabidiol (CBD), a component of marijuana, may be useful for social anxiety, there are also hazards connected with its usage. Be cautious to carefully assess any dangers and advantages when contemplating adopting this as a coping method.

Don't wait too long to get treatment from a mental health professional. While it might be tempting to assume you can tackle this all on your own, frequently individuals require treatment or medication to properly manage social anxiety.

Over time, if you practice relaxation, confront negative ideas, and face fearful events, you will find it easier to control your anxiety in stressful situations. This should assist to ease your social anxiety. However, if you still encounter extreme anxiety on a regular basis, it is vital to visit your doctor or a mental health expert, as conventional treatment such as medication or cognitive-behavioral therapy may be prescribed.

# Chapter 6: Developing Communication Skills for Real life Situations

Building solid connections with other people may considerably lessen stress and worry in your life. In fact, enhancing your social support is connected to greater mental health in general, because having excellent friends may function as a "buffer" for emotions of worry and poor mood. However, for other individuals, their anxiety might contribute to their avoidance of social settings, and hinder them from developing connections. This is particularly true if you are socially nervous and badly want to make friends but are either too frightened to do so or are uncertain about how to reach out to people.

Unfortunately, one of the drawbacks of avoiding social interactions is that you never get the chance to:

Build up your confidence in engaging with others

Develop great communication abilities that would boost the probability of successful partnerships

For example, if you are terrified of going to parties or asking someone out on a date, your lack of experience and/or poor confidence will make it even MORE difficult to know how to handle these circumstances (such as what to dress, what to say, etc). (like what to wear, what to say, etc.). Often, individuals have the required talents but lack the courage to apply them. Either way, practice will boost your confidence and improve your communication abilities.

Why Are Communication Skills Important?

Communication skills are essential to forming (and maintaining) friendships and creating a solid social support network. They also help you take care of your own needs while being sensitive to the needs of others. People aren't born with strong communication skills; like any other ability, they are developed through trial and error and continuous practice.

3 aspects of communication that you may wish to practice are:

Non-verbal communication
Conversation skills
Assertiveness

Note: Of course, there are many parts to good communication and you may require more particular guidance in some areas (e.g. learning how to deal with conflict, presenting skills, providing criticism, etc).

Non-Verbal Communication
A major portion of what we communicate to one another is nonverbal. What you convey to others with your eyes or your body language is equally as powerful as what you express with words. When you feel nervous, you could act in ways that are meant to avoid connecting with people. For example, you may avoid eye contact or talk

extremely quietly. In other words, you are attempting not to communicate, possibly to avoid being assessed badly by others. However, your body language and tone of voice do send important signals to others about your:

Emotional state (e.g. impatience, terror) (e.g. impatience, fear)
Attitude towards the listener (e.g. submissiveness, disdain) (e.g. submissiveness, contempt)
Knowledge of the subject
Honesty (do you have a concealed agenda?)
Thus, if you are avoiding eye contact, standing far away from people, and speaking quietly, you are likely conveying, “Stay away from me!” or “Don’t talk to me!” Chances are, this is not the message that you want to convey.

Conversation Skills
One of the greatest obstacles for someone with social anxiety is beginning conversations and keeping them continuing. It is typical to struggle a little when you are attempting to make small

conversation since it is not always simple to think of things to say. This is particularly true while feeling stressed. On the other side, some worried people speak too much, which may have a bad impact on others.

Assertiveness

Assertive communication is the honest expression of one's own needs, wishes, and sentiments while respecting those of the other person. When you speak assertively, your demeanor is non-threatening and non-judgmental, and you accept responsibility for your actions.

If you are socially anxious, you may have some trouble expressing your ideas and emotions honestly. Assertiveness skills may be tough to develop, particularly when being assertive sometimes involve holding yourself back from the way you would typically do things. For example, you may be terrified of disagreement, constantly go along with the majority, and avoid giving your ideas. As a consequence, you may have acquired a passive communication style. Alternatively, you may seek to control and dominate people and have developed an aggressive communication style.

However, a forceful communication style has numerous advantages. For example, it may assist you to connect to people more truly, with less worry and animosity. It also provides you with greater control over your life and minimizes emotions of powerlessness. Furthermore, it affords OTHER people the right to live their lives.

Barriers to Behaving Assertively - Myths about Assertiveness

MYTH #1: ASSERTIVENESS MEANS GETTING YOUR OWN WAY ALL THE TIME

This is not true. Being assertive implies expressing your point of view and talking honestly with others. Often, you may not get "your own way" when you are assertively offering your views. But expressing to people how you feel and attempting to work out a compromise demonstrates respect for both yourself and others.

## MYTH #2: BEING ASSERTIVE MEANS BEING SELFISH

This is untrue. Just because you voice your thoughts and your preferences do not imply that other people are obligated to go along with you. If you express yourself assertively (not aggressively) then you create a way for others. You may also be forceful on behalf of someone else (e.g. I would prefer Susan to select the restaurant this week) (e.g. I would like Susan to choose the restaurant this week).

## MYTH #3: PASSIVITY IS THE WAY TO BE LOVED

This is untrue. Being passive involves constantly agreeing with others, always allowing them to have their way, yielding to their wants, and having no demands or requests of your own. Behaving this way is no assurance that people will appreciate or admire you. People may regard you as uninteresting and feel annoyed that they can't truly get to know you.

MYTH #4: IT'S IMPOLITE TO DISAGREE

This is not true. Although there are certain occasions when we don't provide our honest view (e.g. most people express how gorgeous a friend looks in her wedding dress, or we only say nice things on the first day of a new job) (e.g. most people say how beautiful a friend looks in her wedding dress, or we only say positive things on the first day of a new job). Much of the time, though, other people will be interested in what you believe. Think how you would feel if everyone constantly agreed with you.

MYTH #5: I HAVE TO DO EVERYTHING I AM ASKED TO DO

False. A major aspect of being forceful is defining and respecting personal limits. This is challenging for many individuals. With our friends, we may fear that they will think we are selfish and uncaring if we don't do all they ask.

At work, we may fear that people will think we are lazy or inefficient if we don't accomplish all we are requested. But other people cannot possibly know how busy you are, how much you despise a specific work, or what other plans you have already made until you tell them. Most people would feel awful to hear that you had done something for them that you didn't have the time for (e.g. drafting a report that needs you to work all weekend) or something you loathe doing (e.g. helping a buddy relocate) (e.g. helping a friend move).

Identifying your problem spots

Below are some questions that you may wish to ask yourself to select the areas you want to improve on:

Do I have problems beginning conversations?
Do I soon run out of things to say?
Do I prefer to say "yes", nod, and attempt to keep other people talking to avoid having to talk?

Am I reluctant to talk about myself?

Tips for Starting a Conversation:

Start a conversation by saying something general and not too personal, for example, talk about the weather ("Gorgeous day, isn't it?"); pay a compliment ("That sweater looks great on you"); make an observation ("I noticed that you were reading a book on sailing, do you have a boat?"); or introduce yourself ("I don't think we have met, I'm…").

You don't need to say something especially funny. It's preferable to be truthful and authentic.

Once you have chatted for a while, particularly if you have known the individual for some time, it could be suitable to go on to more personal topics,e.g relationships; family concerns; personal sentiments; spiritual views; etc.

Remember to pay attention to your nonverbal behavior–make eye contact and talk loudly enough so that people can hear you.

Tips for Keeping a Conversation Going:

Remember that a discussion is a 2-way street — don't speak too little, or too much. As much as feasible, strive to participate in around one-half of the discussion while conversing 1-on-1.

Disclose some personal information about yourself, such as your weekend activities, your preferred hockey team, or a hobby or interest. Personal information does not need to be "too personal"; you may start by sharing your opinion on movies and literature, or talking about activities that you enjoy doing.

Try to exhibit a little vulnerability: it may even be OK to confess that you are a little apprehensive (for example, "I never know what to say to break the ice", or "I'm always so worried at gatherings when I scarcely know anyone"). However, take care – sometimes disclosing too much too soon can put others off.

Ask inquiries about the other person but when you are initially getting to know someone, take care not to ask questions that are too personal. Appropriate inquiries can be to inquire about their weekend activities, their preferences, or their opinion regarding anything you said. For

example, "How do you like that new restaurant?"
Try to ask open-ended questions rather than close-ended inquiries. A close-ended question is answered with a few words, such as yes or no, for example, "Do you enjoy your job?" In contrast, an open-ended question invites much more detail; for example, "How did you get into your line of work?"
Do I talk too much when I'm nervous?
Remember: People generally like to talk about themselves, especially if the other person is showing genuine interest.

Tips for Ending a Conversation:

Remember, all conversations end sometime – don't feel rejected or become anxious as a conversation nears its end. Running out of things to talk about doesn't mean you are a failure or that you are boring.
Think of a gentle approach to finish the discussion. For example, you can say that you need to refill your drink, catch up with another

person at a party, or get back to work, or you can promise to continue the conversation at a later time or date (e.g. "Hope we'll have a chance to chat again," or "Let's have lunch together soon.")

Step 2: Experiment with and practice your conversation skills

The next time you have an opportunity to practice starting or ending a conversation, try breaking some of your normal patterns. For example, if you prefer not to talk about yourself, try to express your ideas and emotions a little more and see what occurs. Or, if you tend to wait for the other person to end the conversation, try a graceful exit yourself first.

Below are a few suggestions for some practice situations:

Speak to a stranger: e.g. at a bus stop, in an elevator, or waiting in line.

Talk to your neighbors: e.g. about the weather or anything going on in the area.

Interact with co-workers: e.g. speak with co-workers during your coffee break or in the staffroom at lunch.

Have friends over for a get-together: e.g. invite a co-worker or acquaintance over, meet someone for coffee, or give a birthday celebration for a relative. Make sure you engage with your visitors.

Try giving a compliment: Resolve to give at least 2 compliments each day – preferably ones that you would not normally give. But remember to always be sincere: only pay a compliment to someone if you truly believe what you are saying.

# Chapter 7: Treatment and Therapy for Social Anxiety Disorder

Various therapy approaches may help individuals control their symptoms, acquire confidence, and conquer their anxiety.

Without therapy, however, social anxiety disorder may remain throughout life – though it may feel better or worse at particular periods.

Healthcare providers will typically prescribe treatment with psychotherapy, medication, or both. The sections following will look at these alternatives in greater depth.

Psychotherapy

Psychotherapy, or talking therapy, helps individuals comprehend their experiences and create appropriate coping mechanisms.

There are various varieties of psychotherapy, including:

CBT\interpersonal treatment
psychodynamic therapy\family therapy
CBT is a frequent therapy. It seeks to assist the individual notice and altering unfavorable attitudes or beliefs about social circumstances. It also seeks to improve people's habits or responses to circumstances that provoke anxiety.

CBT may assist a person to comprehend that their own ideas, not those of others, can affect how they respond and behave.

Exposure therapy, or cognitive administered exposure, may also assist. Alongside this technique, the individual progressively builds up to addressing the events they dread with a therapist in a secure atmosphere.

Medications
A selection of drugs may help patients manage the symptoms of social anxiety disorder.

The three primary categories are antianxiety medicines, antidepressants, and beta-blockers. The sections following will look at these alternatives in greater depth.

Antidepressants

Selective serotonin reuptake inhibitors, which people primarily use as antidepressants, may also assist with the symptoms of social anxiety disorder. They may take many weeks or months to take action.

Some instances include:

paroxetine (Paxil, Paxil CR) (Paxil, Paxil CR)
sertraline (Zoloft) (Zoloft)
fluoxetine (Prozac, Sarafem) (Prozac, Sarafem)

Serotonin-norepinephrine reuptake inhibitors, which are another family of antidepressants, may also aid.

Some instances include:

venlafaxine (Effexor, Effexor XR) (Effexor, Effexor XR)
desvenlafaxine (Pristiq)\duloxetine (Cymbalta) (Cymbalta)

Anti Anxiety medicines
Anti Anxiety medicines function swiftly to alleviate the symptoms of anxiety, but physicians will normally suggest them as short-term therapy since they might cause reliance.

Benzodiazepines are a prevalent class of antianxiety medication. Some examples of these are alprazolam (Xanax) and clonazepam (Klonopin) (Klonopin).

In 2020, the Food and Drug Administration (FDA) enhanced its warning concerning benzodiazepines. Using these medicines may develop a physical dependency, and withdrawal can be life-threatening. Combining them with alcohol, painkillers, and other narcotics may end in death. It is vital to follow the doctor's directions while taking these medications.

Beta-blockers

Beta-blockers help suppress the physical consequences of anxiety, such as perspiration, tremors, and a fast pulse. They achieve this by inhibiting the stimulating effects of adrenaline.

Doctors frequently prescribe these medicines for certain circumstances, such as needing to deliver a presentation, but not for continuing therapy.

Tips for conquering anxiety

Social anxiety is a very personalized experience. The recommendations that benefit one individual may be less useful for another. For this reason, it might be beneficial to explore multiple ways to find out what works best.

The following ideas may help individuals overcome nervousness in social settings.

Increase social situations gradually

People with social anxiety disorder generally avoid social settings where they may provoke their emotions of worry. Although this lessens anxiety in the short term, avoidance may make anxiety considerably worse in the long term.

If feasible — and with the support of a therapist, if required — the individual might gradually increase their exposure to the circumstances they dread. This gives room for them to have a pleasant experience with the scenario.

Having pleasant social interactions may enhance a person's confidence and lower their anxiety or comfort them so that they can overcome it.

Take time to relax

Engaging in mood-boosting activities produces feel-good chemicals in the brain, which may decrease stress and help a person feel better about their emotions of worry.

Before entering into a social scenario that seems frightening, consider doing something calming or pleasurable, such as listening to music, reading, playing a video game, or meditating.

Reframe your thinking

If a person keeps onto the belief that they are shy, it will exacerbate existing worry about talking to others or being in public. Thoughts fuel behavioral patterns.

A strategy connected to CBT includes assisting individuals through the reframing process. Writing down these mental processes might assist.

For example, “I am a shy person” might become “I behaved like a shy person during the gathering.” It may assist the individual to realize that they can modify how they view themselves and how they feel that others see them.

Avoid leaning on booze

Using alcohol and other drugs may decrease anxiety in the short term, but it may make anxiety worse over time and lead to dependency or substance use disorders.

www.ingramcontent.com/pod-product-compliance
Lightning Source LLC
LaVergne TN
LVHW050336160826
845677LV00014B/3638

* 9 7 9 8 3 6 1 1 6 2 8 4 0 *